Old HUNTLY

by
Alan Cooper

The Square was originally the town's market place; fishwives who had travelled from the coast would gather there to sell fish, along with other merchants selling their goods. The feeing markets, at which farmers would hire workers and servants for the following six months, were also held in the Square (and Duke Street). Farm workers were paid when they had completed their six month stint, and in 1918 wages ranged from £14 for boys leaving school, to £25 for lads aged 15 to 20 years, up to £38 for a grieve (foreman). The hiring of women was transferred to register offices in 1899. Peter Fair was an annual market held in July when farmers hired workers for the duration of the harvest, a period of about four to six weeks. The end of the nineteenth century saw a decline in this market, and in 1918, when many men were away fighting in the war, not a single eligible man turned up, and there were only a few farmers.

© Alan Cooper 1999
First published in the United Kingdom, 1999,
by Stenlake Publishing, Ochiltree Sawmill, The Lade,
Ochiltree, Ayrshire, KA18 2NX
Telephone / Fax: 01290 423114

ISBN 1 84033 091 0

FURTHER READING

The books listed below were used by the author during his research. None of them are available from Stenlake Publishing. Those interested in finding out more are advised to contact their local bookshop or reference library.

Barnes, Cyril A., *Huntly, Capital of Strathbogie*, 1998.
Gray, George, *Recollections of Huntly*, 1892.
Macdonald, Greville, *George Macdonald and his Wife*, 1924.
Macdonald, James, *Place Names in Strathbogie*, 1891.
Raeper, William, *George Macdonald*, 1987.
Scott, Patrick W., *Huntly Golf Club, 1892-1992*, 1992.
Scott, Patrick W., *The History of Strathbogie*, 1997.
Scott, Patrick W., *Huntly*, 1999.
Wyness, Fenton, *Let's Look Around the Huntly Area* (no date).
Huntly Express, 1863 onwards (weekly).

Some tinkers in the Huntly area in 1906, photographed by J. Mitchell of Huntly. At the time tinkers were a common sight. On one occasion, in July 1890, a tinker woman was seen lying on the grass of the Market Muir as if asleep. The sight was so common that it did not arouse any suspicion, although later on the woman was found to have died. A favourite camping site for the tinkers was in the Bin Wood. In October 1899, Hugh White, tinsmith, was charged with beating Donald and David Stewart, tinsmiths, over the head with a stick at the camp in the Bin Wood. A good deal of drinking had been going on. White, who could not read or write, pleaded guilty and was fined ten shillings with the option of five days in prison instead.

INTRODUCTION

Huntly, originally in the lands of Strathbogie, owes both its existence and its name to the Gordon family from Berwickshire. In 1696, the Presbytery of Strathbogie included the parishes of Botarie and Ruthen (now Cairnie), Dunbennan and Kinnoir (now Huntly), Glass, Gartly, and Rhynie and Essie (now Rynie). Strathbogie was granted by Robert the Bruce to Adam de Gordon of Berwickshire in 1319, though it was not until 1376 that the family actually settled in the area. They brought the name Huntly with them. It was obviously one that they liked, as when the 2nd Lord Gordon was created an earl in 1445 it was as the 1st Earl of Huntly (and not Strathbogie). The family's base at Strathbogie Castle was renamed Huntly Castle by a charter in 1506. There was no town of Huntly at the time, but two small hamlets existed in the vicinity. The Raws of Strathbogie was a row of houses in the shadow of the castle, from where the golf course is today down towards Old Road. Another hamlet, called Torrisoule, was situated towards the west, possibly near the Torry Road area in modern Huntly. In time, these hamlets grew in size and gradually became the town of Huntly, though some writers continued to use the old names. Torrisoule is mentioned in records until about 1645, while the Raws of Strathbogie was still being referred to in 1727 (though the list of pollable persons, compiled in 1696, refers to the latter as 'Raws of Huntly').

From his base at Strathbogie, the 1st Earl of Huntly became a great force in the north of Scotland. He was granted the Lordship of Badenoch, and also acquired, on the death of his grandmother c.1437, Cluny, Aboyne and Glenmuick. His son, the 2nd Earl, married Princess Arabella, a daughter of James I, and acquired the lands of Boyne, Enzie and Netherdale from the Crown. The 3rd Earl added the Braes of Lochaber to the estates. The family reached the height of its power under the 4th Earl (1513-1562), who was with good reason known as the 'Cock of the North'. He held the title Lieutenant of the North, and was also the Earl of Moray for a time, as well as being Chancellor of Scotland in 1547. He was the wealthiest and most powerful subject in Scotland, and is also said to have been the wisest. However, on Queen Mary's return from France, she and other members of the nobility moved against the Earl when he failed to hand over his son, Sir John, for a minor offence. Instead, Huntly decided to confront his enemies on the battlefield at Corrichie (near Midmar) in 1562. He died from a stroke during the battle, his men were defeated, and seven members of his family, including his son John, were captured and executed in the Castlegate at Aberdeen. Though the Earl had died, his enemies had not yet finished with him and his body was embalmed and transported to Edinburgh where he was put on trial for treason before Parliament. His coffin was propped up so that he was in a standing position, a plea of guilty was entered on his behalf, and his estates were then forfeited.

The power of the Gordons had been temporarily broken, but they recovered quickly when in 1565 Queen Mary restored the Earl's son, George, to the estates,

and he became the 5th Earl of Huntly. This Earl died rather curiously in 1576 while playing football. He is said to have kicked the ball only twice before falling on his face and dying. The 6th Earl, who was created 1st Marquis of Huntly, was head of the Catholic Party in Scotland, and the family remained staunchly Catholic during the religious wars of the seventeenth century. As a result, Huntly Castle, and the district around it, suffered at the hands of the Protestant Government's armies, and the 2nd Marquis was beheaded in Edinburgh in 1649, soon after the execution of Charles I in England.

Following the Restoration of the monarchy in 1660 the next marquis was rewarded for his loyalty, becoming a duke, with the title Duke of Gordon. It was at this time that the family moved to a new main residence, Bog of Gight in Fochabers (afterwards called Gordon Castle), and Huntly Castle was left to decay and disintegrate. In 1715 the Marquis of Huntly, son and heir of the duke, rushed south with his forces to join the Jacobite Rebellion. He fought at Sherriffmuir, but then decided to withdraw to the north, and succeeded to his father's estates the following year.

In 1737, the 3rd Duke of Gordon brought Hugh McVeagh from Belfast to Huntly to promote the linen industry. McVeagh introduced improved spinning wheels and more efficient methods of spinning, weaving and bleaching. He also brought new patterns for napkins, tablecloths and other linen items with him. Houses were built for the weavers, and bleaching fields laid out. The industry prospered to the extent that by 1754 Huntly was producing £40,000 worth of linen annually, and £90,000 worth by 1783, one-fifth of the total production in Scotland. Large quantities were sent to London, Nottingham, Paisley and Glasgow. Linen, and later on cotton, was sent from all over Scotland to be bleached in Huntly. When McVeagh died, the businesses were taken over by one of his employees, Charles Macdonald, and passed to his three sons, George, Charles and James Macdonald in 1819.

The 4th Duke of Gordon raised the Gordon Highlanders regiment in 1794, assisted by his famous wife, Jane, who was known as 'the Flower of Galloway' and 'the beautiful Duchess'. She is reputed to have given recruits a shilling and a kiss, though there is some dispute about whether this story is true. The Duchess certainly rode out to country fairs wearing a Highland bonnet and a regimental jacket. She enjoyed parties and other social events, met Robert Burns, and corresponded with both him and Walter Scott. Seven generations and 200 years later, the lineage of the Duke and Duchess of Gordon led to a famous descendant in Princess Diana. She was descended from their daughter, Charlotte, who married the 4th Duke of Richmond.

Modern Huntly remains a service centre providing shopping and banking facilities for its agricultural hinterland, but the old industries such as linen manufacture are now extinct.

George Arnott came to Huntly in 1869 when he became manager of the tanworks in Church Street. He quickly set up his own business in Granary Street, however, as hide, skin and tallow factor. In 1893 he bought a two acre site which extended from the Square to Chapel Street where he established the Strathbogie Boot Factory in 1897. This employed 150 people, including boys and girls as well as adults. Most were on piecework, but those on set wages went on strike in May 1898. One of their demands was that their hours were reduced from 56 to 54 per week. In July 1896 Huntly's first telephone was installed between the company's offices and their warehouse in Chapel Street. By that time the business was described as a leather merchant's. John A. Dunn's shop, also known as the Globe Boot and Shoe Warehouse, was next door to the Strathbogie Boot Factory. The shop moved to 39 Duke Street in June 1911.

The drinking fountain on the left was gifted by Isabella Robertson in 1882 in memory of her husband, James Robertson, though sadly she died before the opening ceremony. Robertson carried on Huntly Distillery at Pirriesmill and was also a banker in Huntly. The premises of John Wilson, grocer, are on the right. Wilson had worked in the shop as an apprentice when it was owned by John Porter. After spending a year in London, he opened his first shop in Duke Street in 1892, later moving to 37 Duke Street, and relocating to the Square in December 1901. The local press mentioned that his new shop included 'one of Pickering's patent self-sustaining elevators [which] has been placed to run from the cellar to the top storey, four flights in all' (*Huntly Express*, 7 December 1901). Wilson also started a dairy called Strathbogie Dairy and bought the old brewery buildings (see page 27) which he turned into a piggery. In January 1924 he sold the grocery business on the Square to W. J. Howieson, grocer, of Old Road.

The Square and Huntly Hotel, Huntly.

The Square is dominated by a statue of the 5th Duke of Richmond who inherited Huntly from his uncle, the 5th (and last) Duke of Gordon, in 1836. Richmond's youngest daughter, Cecilia, Countess of Lucan, was the grandmother of Cynthia, Countess Spencer, herself grandmother of Princess Diana. As a young man in 1814, the duke fought at Orthez, where he was shot and a bullet became lodged in his chest. This caused serious internal bleeding, and his life was saved by a junior surgeon who opened a vein in his foot, diverting the flow of blood away from his chest. The duke also fought at Waterloo in 1815. The statue in his honour was erected by his tenants in 1862 on the site of an old well.

PROCLAMATION OF KING GEORGE V. AT HUNTLY. MAY 11TH 1910.

PHOTO BY CLARK & SON.

On 11 May 1910, the first ever proclamation ceremony was held in Huntly (previously only royal burghs had been allowed to conduct the ceremony). Following a procession from Stewart's Hall to the Square, the provost read the proclamation from a platform in front of the Duke of Richmond's statue. 'The Territorials then presented arms, and they stood in that position while part of the national anthem was being sung by the scholars under the leadership of Mr Paton, science master . . . then came the cheering for the new king. Territorials and scouts marched past, and the great crowd began to break up. Provost Rhind and the other gentlemen then proceeded to Stewart's Hall, where the three local governing bodies . . . were entertained to a cake and wine banquet, to drink to the health of King George the Fifth.' (*Banffshire Journal*, 17 May 1910.)

In March 1891 the Gordon Arms Hotel was up for sale. It was bought by the then tenant, Mrs Grant, who had come to the hotel in 1861 with her husband, Alexander. He died in 1867 but Mrs Grant continued to run the hotel with the help of her son, Alexander B. Grant. A licence was first granted to Alexander Grant in 1845 when he was tenant of the Strathbogie Hotel. Following Mrs Grant's death in 1896, Alexander Grant carried on the business until 1923 when he retired and sold the hotel to William Pirie, a native of Huntly who was working in Glasgow at the time. The hotel was built c.1820 on a site previously occupied by a heather-roofed building called Mellis's Inn. There is a reference to the inn in 1749 when guests of the Duke of Gordon were recorded as staying there.

Huntly Hotel.

The Huntly Hotel cost £6,000 to build and was opened on Friday 13 July 1900 with a luncheon for forty of the shareholders. Mrs Barclay, formerly of the Gordon Arms Hotel, was appointed as manageress. At the annual general meeting in April 1904 it was reported that there had been a loss of £286 for the year, and that losses since opening totalled £767. An offer of £6,000 for the hotel from John Macdonald of Skye was considered and accepted. Macdonald moved to the Royal Station Hotel, Forres, and leased the Huntly Hotel to various tenants. In 1910 John Halkett took it on a five-year lease, and until 1920 the tenant was G. G. Dow. John Macdonald sold it that year to James Sandison, a son of John Sandison of the Strathbogie Hotel. From about 1924, when it was advertised in the *Huntly Express* that 'Motor 'bus attends all trains', the hotel had its own taxi (above). James Sandison sold the hotel to John Crerar in 1927.

CASTLE STREET, HUNTLY

The Brander Library, right, was gifted to the town by William Brander and was opened on 13 January 1885 by the Earl of Aberdeen. William was the eldest son of George Brander, shoemaker, of 17 Duke Street. On leaving school he joined the Union Bank in Huntly as an apprentice, and worked there for eight years, becoming the accountant at the branch. At the age of 22 he left for London to work for a firm of stockbrokers, and afterwards established his own firm, William Brander & Co., Stockbrokers, of 5 Draper's Gardens, becoming a member of the London Stock Exchange. He died at his residence in Wallington, Surrey, in May 1916, aged 71 years. One of his daughters married William Collins, of the publishing firm. The Huntly Hotel is on the left of the picture.

Gordon Street, Huntly.

James Anderson's grocery shop at 18 & 20 Gordon Street opened for business in 1902, and in 1906 Anderson was advertising tea at 3/- per pound and coffee at 1/8 per pound. Domenico Rizza opened Rizza's Ices, next door, in 1929. The same family opened a fish & chip restaurant at 10 Castle Street in February 1939. The property at the corner with Granary Street was a furniture store owned by W. McKay when it was bought by the Elite Entertainments Syndicate and converted into the Palace cinema, with seating for 300 people. The Palace opened on 3 November 1913, but was closed when its owners opened a new, larger, cinema in 1932. The premises then became a furniture store again, with Robert J. Anton opening for business in May the same year.

Gordon Street and Town Hall, Huntly. 10.

The Palace cinema was opened by Provost Christie on 27 June 1932. The local paper reported 'that the event . . . aroused much interest in the town', and noted that this was evidenced by 'the queue which formed up long ere the ceremony was due to take place, and from the fact that a large number altogether failed in getting admission' (*Huntly Express*, 1 July 1932). The new cinema cost about £10,000 to build and furnish, and could accommodate 450 in the stalls and a further 136 in the balcony. It was an 'all talkies' cinema, and the first film to be shown there was *Congress Dances*, apparently the 'film of the year' at the time. In May 1938, after some alterations and improvements, the cinema was reopened as the Playhouse.

GORDON STREET, HUNTLY.

This picture, dating from *c.*1910, shows James Beattie's grocer's and general merchant's shop at 48 Gordon Street on the left. In March 1925 the tenant of the shop was George Robertson, who had carried on the business for many years. He bought the property, along with an adjoining bakehouse occupied by Mr Murdoch, plus houses at 54 & 56 Gordon Street, and three houses in Upperkirkgate known as Beattie's Buildings. From 1919 onwards the shop on the right at the corner (with a sign for John Simpson), was occupied by Charles Anderson, butcher and poulterer. Huntly and District Ex-Service Men's Club (originally the Discharged Sailors' and Soldiers' Association) was formed in the same building at the end of the First World War, and in 1923 bought the premises from the Duke of Richmond.

This Salvation Army harvest festival picture was taken in 1912 by Kilgour, studio photographer, of 57 Bogie Street. The officers in Huntly at that time were Capt. John Dempsey and Lieut. William Ackerley. The Salvation Army came to Huntly in May 1903 and the original officers remained in the town until July 1904 when they changed places with those at Dunoon. In August 1906 William Booth, founder of the Salvation Army, and popularly known as 'General' Booth, visited Huntly. He delivered an address in the United Free Church (now Strathbogie Church) on the subject of 'The Salvation Army: Past, Present and Future'. General Booth said that the Salvation Army 'was a band of godly men and women banded together to deal with the classes steeped in misery, drink and vice' (*Huntly Express*, 3 August, 1906). The address took place during a violent thunderstorm with flashes of lightning. Afterwards, General Booth was the guest of Bailie and Mrs Donald, of Springbank. As the cars moved off to Inverurie, General Booth was cheered by a large crowd.

This postcard was sent from Huntly to Banff in December 1904 with the message: 'I hope you will like this one, it is one of our football club'. It probably refers to a junior team called Huntly Wanderers which was formed in January 1904. Football was a popular game in Huntly in the nineteenth century, and there were various attempts to bring some organisation to the sport. On 8 November 1884 the *Huntly Express* reported that: 'A meeting of the Huntly Football Club was held in the Temperance Hotel on Monday evening when the following office-bearers were appointed for the season—viz:- captain, Mr W. J. Macdonald; vice-captain, Mr J. Spence Legge; secretary and treasurer, Mr T. A. Duff; committee, Messrs D. McGlashan, W. Aitchison, J. Smith and R. McGregor.' This club must have had a brief existence as in September 1890 some people met in Gordon's Temperance Hotel and set up another team, also called Huntly Football Club. The team became known as Huntly United following its amalgamation with another team in the 1890s.

Huntly Jubilee Cottage Hospital was built in the years 1888-89 at a cost of £1,257 and consisted of four wards, each with four beds. It was opened on 18 September 1889 by the Duke of Richmond, in a ceremony at Stewart's Hall, when a two-day bazaar was held to raise money for the hospital's endowment fund. This raised the remarkable sum of £853, and the first patient was admitted on 4 December 1889. In the first year to October 1890, 62 patients were treated, of whom 7 died, 9 remained in hospital, and the rest were discharged. The first matron, Mary Barclay, originally from Marnoch, died tragically at the age of 65 after working for eighteen years at the hospital, having contracted blood-poisoning after pricking her finger on a fish bone. The amputation of the infected finger failed to save her life.

In January 1893 the Royal Oak Hotel was owned by Mrs Grant of the Gordon Arms. At that point her tenant, Mrs Rae, bought the Strathbogie Hotel, and a new tenant, Alexander Raeburn, came to the Royal Oak on an eleven year lease. Alterations and improvements made at the time included the addition of a new bar and extra bedrooms. The hotel had stable accommodation and a hiring department, and Mr Raeburn announced in the local paper that he had added a new landau to the hotel's fleet of vehicles. William Berry was the tenant from March 1904 until 1920, when he retired and went to live at Dyce. The next tenant was William Rennie of Aberdeen.

Duke Street, Huntly.

Looking down Duke Street towards Bogie Street, with the house where George Macdonald was born on the right. John B. Singer, whose shop was at number 41a, was a fruiterer, confectioner and florist. In past centuries, traders and shopkeepers were grouped under the general term 'merchants'. In 1696, a list was made of all inhabitants aged 16 and over in the parish of Dunbennan for the poll tax (Huntly and the surrounding area was part of this parish at the time). The list included 10 merchants. The vast majority of people were either tenant farmers (67), farm workers (136), or servants (115). Other occupations included 'herds' (22), weavers (12), millers (6), masons (5), shoemakers (4), glovers (4), harvest hooks (3), smiths (2), and tailors (2). Surprisingly, none of the following were mentioned: teachers, ministers, or doctors. In 1696 there were 269 men and 247 women aged 16 or over in the parish.

Dawson & Company's Emporium at 57 Duke Street was run by Robert Dawson for 33 years before being taken over by his son, Robert Alexander Dawson, in November 1909. The emporium sold clothes, as well as other goods including curtains and linoleum. The next shop along was occupied by James Scott, butcher. On 3 September 1909 the *Huntly Express* reported that 'while a quantity of meat was being delivered at the shop from Mr Scott's spring cart, the pony turned sharply round and backed into the window, completely smashing it'.

BOGIE STREET, HUNTLY

The Loggie Buildings, on the right, were designed by T. F. Archibald and built in the years 1906-07 for William Loggie, with two shops on the ground floor and dwelling-houses above. The foundation stone was laid in November 1906 with full Masonic honours in a ceremony which included a procession from Meadow Street to Bogie Street headed by a pipe band, with the principal officers bringing up the rear. At Bogie Street a special platform was erected for the ladies. The first tenants in the shops were Robert Duffton, chemist, in the nearest one, and William A. Ingram, draper, in the other. The latter business was taken over by G. B. McCartney in July 1926 but continued to trade as 'The Balcony Drapery Warehouse'.

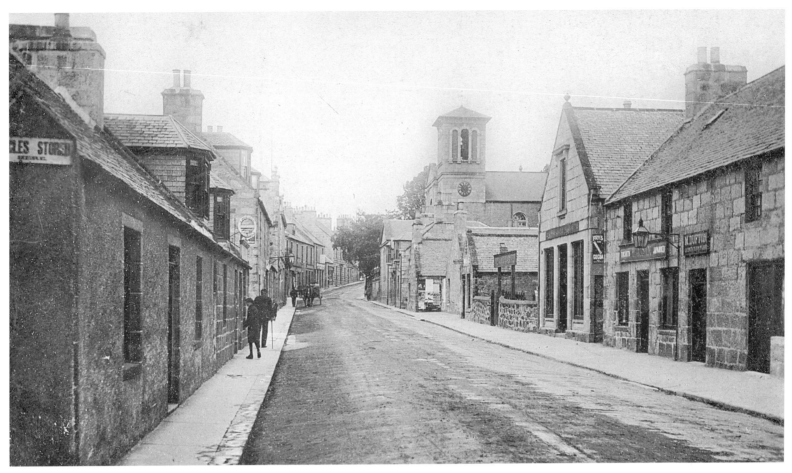

Bogie Street, with the shops of M. Dufton and William J. Sim on the right. The latter, a tinsmith and japanner, bought the business in September 1903 from William Wilson, tinsmith, who had carried on the business for 8 years. Mr Sim had previously been employed for 22 years by J. Bowman & Son, lamp manufacturers. He was also an artist and executed commissions for illuminated addresses and similar work. He was an active man in the local community, being secretary to several organisations including the cricket club, the Lodge of Freemasons, and the Lodge of Free Gardeners (a friendly society). He died in 1917 aged 51 years. The Free Church, in the centre of the picture, became the United Free Church in 1900.

The Bridge of Bogie was originally a steep, humpback bridge, probably like the one that can still be seen in Keith. This was replaced in about 1807 with a bridge that was suitable for mail-coaches and other vehicles. In 1895 it was widened by removing the parapets and laying girders at each side, providing room for pavements six feet wide. The reopening ceremony was performed by Mrs Bisset of Lessendrum, who declared the bridge open and then cut a red silk ribbon with a pair of silver scissors. The Huntly Volunteers Band under Mr Diveri occupied a position near the centre of the bridge. Children had a holiday in the afternoon so that they could attend and shops were closed for several hours during the event. Afterwards, a banquet was held in Stewart's Hall.

The mill at Bogie Bridge, owned by Messrs A. & F. Stephen and usually called Stephen's Mill, was closed down in 1954 and now no trace of it remains. In 1892 a fire was reported in the local paper: 'On a search being made, it was seen that the fire had broken out in the teasing-room, and had been caused by friction and the igniting of a quantity of wool' (*Huntly Express*, 30 April 1892). Working at the mill could be dangerous, especially for the young and careless. In July 1916 Maggie Clark, aged 15, was operating a scouring machine when she allowed her right hand to be caught in the rollers. Another worker stopped the machine quickly by knocking off the driving belt, preventing an even more serious injury. As it was, her right had was so badly damaged that it had to be amputated by doctors at the Jubilee Hospital.

A postcard dated 1909 showing a view taken from the Bogie Bridge. In the late autumn people would gather on the bridge to watch salmon negotiating the salmon ladder; some even took the opportunity to rush into the water and grab a fish, making a very easy catch. The edge of the dye-works is to the right. These were once part of Stephen's Mill, but were taken over in 1908 by Mr Castell who had been the manager for the previous seven years. In November 1916 the local paper reported that rod fishing on the Bogie and Deveron at Huntly had ended in October, and that over 100 salmon had been caught at Huntly compared to about 70 the previous year.

Scott's Hospital, also known as Scott's Institution, was opened on 1 August 1855, and usually had 20 to 30 residents during the nineteenth century. Its founder, Dr Alexander Scott, a native of Huntly, had died in 1833 and left his wealth (which included the estate of Craibstone) to be used after his wife's death for the building and endowment of a hospital for the old people of Huntly. The hospital (essentially an old folks' home) burned down ten years after it opened, but was rebuilt, and new wings were completed in 1899 following a bequest from Alexander Morison of Bognie. Morison was born in 1809 on the island of Tobago. His father, James, was the inventor of 'Morison's Vegetable and Universal Medicine', commonly known as 'Morison's Pills'. As a young man, Alexander served in a regiment of the East India Company, and afterwards joined the family pill business in London. He inherited Bognie and Frendraught estates from a relative in 1874, and died in 1879. Scott's Hospital was extended following his wife's death in 1893.

Looking down on Gladstone Road from Scott's Hospital towards Huntly Bowling and Tennis Club, with Clashmach in the background. The club was formally opened on 25 June 1880, and 'at that time the green was on a site now occupied by Cluny House . . . Four years later we removed to our present green' (*Huntly Express*, 13 November 1931). The pavilion was built in 1886, and was extended in 1899 when water, gas, and heating were installed. George Arnott, president, remembered 'the first green the Huntly bowlers had, which was like some other greens rather bumpy and stotty' (*Huntly Express*, 13 May 1899). The pavilion was extended in 1914 when its length was doubled, and was enlarged again in 1929 when the central part was improved and made more symmetrical.

William Macdonald, born in 1780, and an uncle of the author George Macdonald, converted some disused bleachworks buildings into a brewery early in the nineteenth century. When William J. Macdonald, possibly a son of the founder, retired in 1897, the brewery was bought by F. W. Palmer of Aberdeen, who renovated the premises and added a malting department. The firm's speciality at the time was Strathbogie Stout; lemonade was another product. For some reason the business went into a decline and was closed down, though it was still operating in 1903 when five local men were prosecuted and fined for breaking in and stealing, during two visits, seven gallons of beer and stout. The brewery was run by William Smith at the time. In 1896 there had been a fatal accident when James Ogg of 100 Gordon Street, employed as a bottler, fell from a gangway into the mill race, where his body was found soon afterwards, having stopped the waterwheel from turning.

Hugh McVeagh had been brought to Huntly from Belfast by the 3rd Duke of Gordon because of his expertise in the linen industry. When McVeagh died, the threadworks and bleachfields that he had run were taken over by one of his employees, Charles Macdonald. Following Macdonald's death in 1819, the businesses passed to his sons George, Charles and James (the eldest son, William, started a successful brewery on his own). As the threadworks and bleachfields became unprofitable and were closed down, the brothers turned to other enterprises, including making flour and starch from potatoes, but this venture ceased with the potato famine of the 1840s. Charles was also a banker in Huntly but through unwise loans got heavily into debt and fled to America, abandoning his wife and two daughters. He died in 1836, aged 41. George and James took over the repayment of their brother's debts, amounting to £6,000, though they were not obliged to do so. The starch mill was converted into a successful meal mill (above), and carried on by James on his own from 1858, and then by his son, also called James, from 1877. The latter was author of *Place Names in Strathbogie* (1891) and *Place Names in West Aberdeenshire* (1899).

In November 1889 twelve to fourteen people were injured, some seriously, when a train from Elgin ran into a stationary train from Aberdeen at Huntly Station. Both were due in to Huntly Station at 8.13 p.m., but should not have been on the same track. Pointsman John Wilkie, aged 24, was arrested. The accident led to some improvements being made, with a cabin erected near the station to observe southbound trains, and another (above) put up in February 1890 at the gates near The Farm for northbound trains. The old level-crossing gates were removed and new ones, operated by levers in the cabin, were installed. There were several tragedies at the crossing, however, including two separate incidents in 1909. Grace Hume, aged about 27, and employed as a milliner in Duke Street, was run over and killed, as was Jessie McGregor, Princes Street, aged 18 years, who was knocked over and decapitated. In 1929 a labourer, Alexander Craigie of 7 West Park Street, had his leg completely severed, and died afterwards in hospital.

This picture shows the house known as The Farm where George Macdonald spent his childhood. Though he never made much money from writing, Macdonald was a popular author during his own lifetime. Queen Victoria was one of his admirers and gave a copy of his novel *Robert Falconer* to each of her grandsons. George often came back to Huntly, to stay with relatives at The Farm, to lecture, and to preach. In September 1890 he gave a lecture on Robert Burns in Stewart's Hall. He held what was virtually a mystical power over his audience, addressing them as 'friends' rather than 'ladies and gentlemen'. He also preached in Huntly, both in the Parish Church and the Congregational Church, and people came from Macduff, Turriff, and other towns to hear him. On one occasion he was due to preach but had a serious nosebleed and Rev. John Pillans had to take his place. In the summer of 1898, George Macdonald suffered a stroke and never wrote another book. He required constant nursing until his death in 1905.

Looking towards Huntly Creamery from near The Farm. The creamery made butter and cheese, and was officially opened on 12 July 1899 by Mr A. M. Gordon of Newton, with 150 people attending the ceremony. It was owned by the Northern Creameries Company Ltd, which had hoped to raise £10,000 in £1 shares, and whose directors included William Sellar, Francis Watt, and William Mellis. The first four years were very difficult, with three returning a loss and the best year only showing a profit of £11, with the result that no dividends were paid to the shareholders. In 1903, at the annual general meeting, the directors complained about the limited supply of milk coming in from farms. The company also had bank borrowings of £2,878, which must have been a great burden in interest payments. By July 1909, when a break-in was reported in the press, the creamery had ceased to be a public company, and was in the ownership of Messrs G. Mellis & Son Ltd.

The Drill Hall cost £2,000 and was opened on 18 November 1902 with speeches by Col. Jackson and Major Mellis. It was built for the 'A' Company of the 4th Volunteer Battalion of the Gordon Highlanders, usually known as the Huntly Volunteers. The six volunteer battalions of the Gordon Highlanders were the 1st/2nd (Aberdeen), 3rd (Peterhead), 4th (Donside), 5th (Deeside), and 6th (Keith). Volunteers engaged in route marching and tactical exercises, and joined their battalion in camp once a year. During the year prizes were awarded for shooting and drill attendance. The Drill Hall contained recreation and reading rooms, and courses in gymnastics, which were free to all members of the company, were held there. In 1895 the Huntly Volunteers had 115 members. The name was changed to the Territorial Force in 1908, and later on to the Territorial Army.

DEVERON STREET, HUNTLY.

The shop on the left, called The Enterprise, was situated at 26 Deveron Street until 1909. It was a drapery and furniture store, which also sold wallpaper. An article in the local paper in 1909 entitled 'Huntly Sixty Years Since' (by A. J.) relates an example of 'riding the stang', when townspeople would seize someone and carry out their own form of punishment on them: 'In Deveron Street lived a fellow called Brown, notorious for ill-using a poor delicate wife. One night about twelve o'clock two men appeared at his bedside, took him out of his bed as he was, and down the street where several stout women were waiting with a strong paling bar and two men with lighted torches. Brown was mounted, and the women marched him across the Square and down Duke Street as far as the Royal Oak, where the men held him under the pump and the women pumped on him till they were tired. He disappeared from the town next day.' (*Huntly Express*, 15 January 1909).

The site that St Margaret's Roman Catholic Church was built on was purchased for £106 in 1832, and had previously been occupied by the Lodge of the local Freemasons. During the eighteenth century, Catholics had worshipped at Robieston Church, but this had been burned during the '45 rebellion. A significant proportion of the funds required to build St Margaret's (above) came from members of the Gordon family who had settled in Spain and left bequests for the building of a church in Huntly. They also gifted seven oil paintings to the church during the 1840s. St Margaret's was opened on 31 August 1834, and is said to have been the first Catholic church in Scotland to have been built with a bell-tower since the Reformation. The church had seating for 400 people. A Catholic school was established next to the church in 1848, and remained in use until 1969.

The foundation stone of the Gordon Schools was laid on 27 February 1839 and they were opened in 1841. Four schools were housed within the one building, each under different control. These were the Established Church School for boys (ground floor, west side), Free Church School for boys (first floor, west side), the Infants School (ground floor, east side) and an Industrial School for girls, one of the first in the country, where girls were taught to cook, knit and sew, as well as to read and write. The building was designed by Archibald Simpson and built as a lasting memorial to the 5th (and last) Duke of Gordon by his widow. It cost about £3,000. The four separate schools were unified in 1888.

This extension to the secondary school cost between £5,000 and £6,000 and was opened on 10 September 1912 by the Duke of Richmond. An increase in the number of pupils had been the main impetus behind building it. In 1895 there had been 70 pupils in the secondary department but by 1912 the numbers had risen to 200. The new building had two classrooms, two science laboratories and a library on the ground floor, plus a corridor connecting it to the existing school building. There were another two classrooms and a large room for instruction in art on the first floor. In the room devoted to classics there were busts of Julius Caesar and Augustus, and a Parthenon frieze. The next major extensions to the schools, opened on 8 May 1958, included an assembly hall and new primary school.

This primary school was opened on 12 September 1904 by Sir Henry Craik, Secretary of the Scottish Education Department. Designed by architect R. G. Wilson of Aberdeen, it contained nine classrooms. There was accommodation for 540 pupils, with a gymnasium that could take another 180 pupils if required. The increase in the school leaving age to 14 had led to a rise in the number of pupils, and the pressure on space was increased further by the Education Department, which wished to subdivide classes. With the construction of a new primary school in recent decades, this building has been turned into a community centre called The Linden Centre.

Club House, Golf Course, Huntly

Huntly Golf Club's clubhouse was opened on 12 March 1908 by General Gordon of Culdrain. Designed by Mr Corrigal, architect, of Keith, it had separate rooms for ladies and gentlemen, with lockers, and a tea-room for the use of the ladies at one corner. Initially there was no water supply, and it was six months before the club decided that they needed one. The club was founded in 1892 and its nine-hole course was designed by Tom Morris. Golf was only played during the winter as from April to September the grass was too long. The club did employ a horse-mower one year, but in 1906 decided to let the course for grazing sheep. T. S. Watt's round of 35 in July 1909 included a 7, but still beat Archie Simpson's record score of 37. The club had its first profitable year in 1910, showing a £5 profit, and membership increased from 109 to 145, the increase being mainly in the ladies section.

PADDLING POOL · COOPER PARK · HUNTLY

The paddling pool during the 1950s. This site is now occupied by the new golf clubhouse, opened in 1988.

In May 1919 a meeting took place in the Good Templar Hall, McVeagh Street, with the purpose of setting up a company of girl guides in Huntly. There was a large turnout of girls at the meeting, and a committee was formed with Mrs B. M. Aitchison, Coniecleugh, as district commissioner. In March 1927 a hut was built for the girl guides in West Park Street, opposite St Margaret's Church. This picture, with Huntly Castle in the background, was probably taken in the 1920s. (Names extracted from the *Huntly Express*, 18 March 1988.)

Back row: Agnes Dean, Julie Masson, Mary Morrison, unknown, Ena Loggie, Jean Rose, Ailsa Gilchrist, Mary Castle, Jess McLennan, Mary Wren, Edith Lobban, Marjorie Philip, Marion Ingram.

Second row: Annabel Shearer, Margaret Watson, Gertie Cruickshank, Lottie Robertson, Mary Symon, Daisy Taylor, Agnes Pirie, Nellie Nicol, Bessie King, Nettie Gauld, Mollie Duncan, unknown, Jean Brander, Margaret Brown.

Third row: Miss Sellar, Grace Lobban, Mary Symon, Flo Milne, Dora Diamond, Nettie Stronach, unknown, Mary Sandison, Mrs Aitchison, Jean Barclay, Isobel McPherson, Mary Reid, ? Ogg, Dolly Murray, Elma Harper, ? Clark, ? Ingram, Miss Wilson.

Front row: Jean Ewan, Daisy Dawson, Betty Mearns, Barry Smith.

Strathbogie Lodge of Oddfellows was formed in 1882 and was part of Keith District, the largest district in the order, extending from Kintore in the south to Stornoway in the west, with 4,000 members divided into about 30 lodges. In 1895 Strathbogie Lodge had 230 members, and had paid out £108 in sickness benefits the previous year. At their annual meeting in Stewart's Hall in 1895 (reported in the *Huntly Express* of 2 February), George Arnott said that 'to be an Oddfellow is for a working man to set himself above being a pauper, and to give him that honest feeling that if trouble overtakes him, what he has stored up by membership with his Lodge will be available in the time of need'. In June 1916 the meetings of the Annual Moveable Committee were held in Huntly, and 117 delegates attended from Scotland, England and Wales. This postcard was produced to commemorate the event. The week began on the Sunday with a procession consisting of the delegates and members of other friendly societies, accompanied by the provost, magistrates, and other officials of the town council, from Bogie Bridge to the Parish Church.

Huntly Castle. In 1314, following a quarrel, Robert the Bruce (King Robert I) confiscated the estates and titles of 'David of Strabolgi', 10th Earl of Atholl, and Strathbogie was given to Sir Adam de Gordon of Berwickshire in 1319. The Gordons replaced the original wooden castle with one made of stone and lime, notable for its deep and dark dungeon, said to have been one of the most unpleasant in Scotland. The castle was rebuilt from the ground upwards between 1551 and 1554 by the 4th Earl of Huntly, but the basement and dungeon were left intact. The 1st Marquis of Huntly added another storey at the beginning of the seventeenth century, with the elaborate dormers, carvings and heraldic designs that are some of the most outstanding features of the castle. In 1647, during the religious wars, Irish troops guarding the castle were captured and hanged; their commander, James Gordon of Newton, who had been left in charge of the castle, was hanged in Edinburgh as a traitor.

Huntly Volunteers Pipe Band, featured on a postcard sent in 1905. Very little about the band has been recorded, but in 1898 the volunteers were advertising for three pipers and the local paper mentioned that a pipe band had been formed in May 1899. Another reference to the band appears in February 1901: 'We do not forget the excellent service which, for a season or two past, has been rendered by the pipe band' (*Huntly Express*, 8 February 1901). A further reference, soon afterwards, was in relation to a new tune called *Huntly's Gallant Volunteers, 1900-1901*: 'The local volunteer pipe band will be glad to get this tune for use in the drill season' (*Huntly Express*, 15 March 1901). The tune was composed by piper Thomas Stone of Fort George. Prior to joining the army, Stone had been employed at Bogie Bridge Mills.

In November 1850 the Great North of Scotland Railway announced that it would proceed with the construction of a line from Kittybrewster in Aberdeen to Keith. However, a shortage of money delayed the project and the company then decided to build the line only as far as Huntly. The first sod was cut on 25 November 1852 at Westhall, Oyne, on property owned by Sir James Elphinstone, chairman of the GNSR. The line opened to goods trains on 12 September 1854, and was officially opened on 19 September, with passenger traffic beginning the next day. On the opening day, a special train ran from Aberdeen carrying 400 passengers and picking up more along the line. It arrived in Huntly, where celebrations were held in a large marquee near the station, with about 650 people on board. Kennethmont Station (above) opened in 1854 but was closed in the 1960s. Surprisingly, the building has survived, but it is in a deteriorating condition.

Amazingly, two Gartly stationmasters were run over and killed in their own station. In April 1917 Alexander Garden was killed when crossing from one platform to another. He came out from behind a passenger train from Keith, and stepped in front of a goods train from Aberdeen. Then in May 1924 his successor, John Geddes, fell on to the rails and was run over by several waggons while supervising shunting operations. These were just two of the many accidents at the station. In 1895 Robert Stuart, farmer at Wraes, Kennethmont, tried to board a train as it was moving away, but fell under it. His legs were crushed, a doctor was summoned, and he was eventually taken to hospital in Huntly, but died. In 1891 a farm worker at Mosstown, Kennethmont, on finding that his train did not stop in Kennethmont, jumped out at Gartly when the train was still moving and hit his head against the southbound train he was rushing to board.

Gartly Picnic and Games was an annual event at the turn of the century, held at various sites in the area. In 1898 the venue was a field at Culdrain, which was lent by Lieut-Col. Gordon. The event that year included bicycle races and a tug-of-war competition in the evening. In 1902 the picnic and games was held in a field near the Central School, on the farm of Collithie. From 1904 it was often held in a field near Bogieside.

Raws of Noth is an interesting hamlet that has completely disappeared during the twentieth century. Though situated near the village of Gartly, close to the farm of Old Noth, the Raws of Noth was actually in the parish of Rhynie. In William M. Alexander's *The Place-Names of Aberdeenshire* (1952), it is described as 'an extinct hamlet'. Some of the gravestones at Rhynie cemetery identify people who lived in the hamlet, including: 'William Balgowan, late in Raws of Noth, who died 22nd November 1809, aged 49 years'; and Robert Glass who 'died at Raws of Noth, 9th August 1879, aged 67 years'. The inscription on another stone reads: 'John Riddel, Raws of Noth, in memory of his daughter, Margaret Riddel, who died there 28th February 1895, aged 28 years'.

Lessendrum House was completely destroyed by fire on 12 January 1928, though many of its contents, including two paintings by Van Dyck, were saved. The fire started in some heating apparatus and quickly got out of control. Aberdeen Fire Brigade was contacted but replied that they could only operate within twenty miles of the city (Lessendrum was forty miles away). Huntly Fire Brigade attended the scene but didn't have a fire engine, and as there was no water pump at the scene, nor even a suitable supply of water, little could be done other than to rescue as many of the valuable contents as possible. Two maids, Nettie Gigg and Bessie Sharp, had to jump 20 to 30 feet into a sheet to escape the blaze; the first was caught but the second fell through the sheet to the ground, although she was only slightly injured. Lessendrum had been the home of the Bisset family from the year 1252, and twenty generations of the family lived there. After the fire they lived in Huntly, and for a time at Rothiemay. They returned to live on the 450-acre estate in 1958, but it was sold in 1981.